MW01672224

A
a
b
iv
SMÅRG

THE GOBLIN COMPANION

A Field Guide to Goblins

Invented and Illustrated by

Brian Froud

Captured and Catalogued by

Terry Jones

BARNES & NOBLE BOOKS
NEW YORK

Copyright © 1986 by Henson Associates, Inc.

Character names are trademarks of Henson Associates, Inc.

All rights reserved. No part of the contents of this book may be reproduced or utilized in any form or by any means, electronic or mechanical, including photocopying, recording, or by any information storage and retrieval system, whithout the written consent of the publisher.

This edition published by Barnes & Noble, Inc.
by arrangement with Pavillion Books Limited

1998 Barnes & Noble Books

ISBN 0-7607-1108-9

M10987654321

First published in Great Britain in 1996 by
Pavillion Books Limited

Designed by Wherefore Art?

Printed and bound in Italy

For Jim Henson,
who led us through
the Labyrinth

Introduction

A LITTLE OVER TEN YEARS AGO (longer if you're reading this *after* I've written it, which is pretty likely to be the case unless you happen to be a foregoblin*) a small, brown, earthenware pot was discovered in a remote corner of the Olduvai Gorge in northern Tanzania. The pot was similar in size and shape to some of the early Egyptian funerary vases dating from 3000 B.C., but—and this was the astonishing fact—it was embedded in the sedimentary rock itself, which dated back at least 60 million years—long before any human life existed on this planet!

The sheer implausibility of such a find so confounded the archaeologists who stumbled upon it that they decided to ignore it. Indeed, they were so perturbed by the whole idea (and by the possibility of having to throw away years of archaeological research) that they didn't even open the pot up to see what was inside. Instead, the pot was discreetly abandoned near some half-full dustbins in the Shimanze district of Mombasa. And it was here that it was eventually discovered by dustmen, some twenty years later.** The dustmen in turn handed it to the only man with professional qualifications who happened to be passing by at the time. This man was Brian Froud—an eccentric piscepodiatrist† who was then scouring the Great Rift Valley in East Africa for work (and not having much success). He had managed to treat a couple of sardines for verrucae, but had received no remuneration from either (since they were both dead) when he made the discovery that was to change his life.

**Foregoblins*: These curious beasts are blessed (or, rather, cursed) with extreme *predictability* (i.e., the ability to predict). They are usually totally ignorant of anything once it's happened, but appear to know everything that hasn't happened yet. The burden of this overwhelming amount of prior knowledge makes the foregoblins restless and unhappy and prone to make the most obvious blunders (because they *know* they're going to). At the same time, of course, they display a total inability to learn from their mistakes or even those of other goblins.

**The writer is aware that there is a discrepancy between the dating of the original discovery of the pot, ten years prior to the time of writing, and its rediscovery twenty years later, but he would like to point out that in geological time accuracy to within even a few million years is considered pretty good, and here it's only a quibble over a measly ten years, and, quite honestly, if you're going to worry about footling little points like that, you might as well give up reading this here and now and good riddance as far as I'm concerned. It's all very well for you readers—*you* can pick and choose which authors you're going to read—but us authors have no say in the matter—*we* have to put up with any Tom, Dick, or Harry picking up our work and running their eyes over it, perusing it, riffling through it—even *thinking* about it and doing anything else they damn well want to with it! Well ... let me tell you! I didn't spend fourteen years at Author Training School just so that any riffraff off the street could paw through my words and spill coffee on them and ... anyway, as this is only a footnote I suggest you stop wasting your time on it and get on with the real introduction.

Oh, by the way, the writer would also like to make it clear that the time lapse between the abandoning of the pot near the dustbins in the Shimanze district and its rediscovery twenty years later (which is nothing in geological time) is in no way meant to be a slur on, nor imply neglect on behalf of the Mombasa North West Garbage Disposal Authority, which is a fine body and has a splendid record of civic enterprise and responsibility.

†*Piscepodiatrist*: A foot doctor who specializes in the treatment of fish.

At first, he thought the pot was merely some 3000-year-old Egyptian funerary vase (see above) and was about to smash it against a wall when he noticed some minute rune-like characters engraved on the underside edge of the rim. From his rudimentary knowledge of runic inscriptions, and using a lot of guesswork, he worked out that the message read: "This is *not* a 3000-year-old Egyptian funerary vase. Please do not smash." He at once realized that the inscription must have been the work of a foregoblin, who had prognosticized this very scene.

Now it so happened that, as well as being a piscepodiatrist (see footnote 3, page 6), Froud was also an eminent goblinologist. He therefore rightly guessed that he was holding in his hands the most important communication between the goblin world and ours to be found in this millennium.

Imagine, then, his excitement as he hurried back to his clapboard room in the Ushirombo Hilton. His fingers were shaking as he opened the sealed urn (the natural consequence of five bottles of Pouilly Fuissé the night before). He lifted off the ancient pottery lid and felt inside for the contents.... There was a click and a snap, and Froud screamed with horror as a 60-million-year-old mousetrap clamped itself onto his fingers!* Yes! It was a typical goblin practical joke, and one which had caught out the eminent goblinologist perfectly. The foregoblin who had set it must have laughed himself silly, seeing in advance (as he would have done) the expression that convulsed Froud's face as he wrenched the contraption off his bleeding fingers. Furious, Froud seized up the pot and was just about to smash it against the wall when he realized it was not empty! There was something else in the very bottom. Eagerly he reached in and ... yes! It was another mousetrap! The foregoblin who set it would have collapsed in a helpless, gibbering heap at this point, whilst without more ado, Froud smashed the pot against the wall. It was only then that he noticed the inscriptions on the underside of each mousetrap. Peering through a haze of freshly drunk Puligny-Montrachet, he deciphered the following messages. On the first trap he read:

you would know of the Labyrinth, Old Man of the Crater.

and on the second:

Stranger! If the Goblins seek the Ngorongoro

**Mousetrap*: Yes, I know mice probably didn't evolve for another 58 million years (during the Quaternary Cenozoic period), but don't forget that this was all the work of a foregoblin, and, anyway, in geological terms what's a mere 58 million years between friends?

After some thought and a couple of bottles of expensive Corton-Charlemagne, he realized that there were not two messages but one, and that by reversing the order in which he read the mousetraps the message ran:

"Stranger! If the Goblins seek the Ngorongoro, you would know of the Labyrinth, Old Man of the Crater." But the meaning still proved elusive.

Firstly, why address the reader as "Stranger!" at the beginning of the message, and then as "Old Man of the Crater" at the end? Secondly, if the pot had indeed been left by a foregoblin, the foregoblin would have known that the pot was going to be found by Froud and not by an "Old Man of the Crater." Fourthly, what was the Ngorongoro, and why should the goblins seek it? And thirdly, why would the "Old Man of the Crater" get to know about the Labyrinth (whatever that was) *only* if the goblins should seek the Ngorongoro?

Frustrated and confused, Froud continued to puzzle over the cryptic message for glass after glass. Two *extremely* expensive bottles of Gevrey-Chambertin and a couple of cases of slightly less expensive but still pricey Pernand-Vergelesses* later, he was still no nearer a solution. Finally he sank into a slumber from which he was to awaken next morning with a cry of "Ekaeur!" (He had meant to cry "Eureka!" but the second case of Pernand-Vergelesses had taken its toll.) During his sleeping hours a thought of breathtaking brilliance had seeped through to his brain. Leaping slowly and carefully out of bed, Froud staggered across to the two mousetraps and with shaking hands (of course) placed them *side by side.* He had done it! The message suddenly became clear. It read:

Stranger! If	*you would know*
the Goblins	*of the Labyrinth,*
seek the	*Old Man of the*
Ngorongoro	*Crater.*

Of course! Why hadn't he thought of it before? (Pretty obvious really, considering most decent white burgundies are about 13 percent in alcoholic strength by volume....) The Ngorongoro Crater was a world-famous landmark and nature reserve, which had been declared a conservation area in 1956. Its grass plains and mountainous moorlands, interspersed by thornbush and rain forest, are the haunt of rhinoceros, elephant, buffalo, leopard, mountain reedbuck, and giant forest hog.

**Pernand-Vergelesses*: One of the lesser known appellations from the Côte de Beaune, Pernand produces mainly red wines with an excellent reputation, but it also produces some of the delicate white wines favoured by Froud.

Without more ado, Froud ran the 250 miles to the Crater and checked into the Ngorongoro Hilton. There, in the bar, he began what promised to be a long series of inquiries to find the whereabouts of the mysterious Old Man of the Ngorongoro Crater—if indeed he existed at all. But here, by pure chance, luck appeared to be running his way for once. It turned out that the barman was 60 million years old and could remember far back to long vanished times when there were not even any Hilton hotels—well, not that many, anyway. He told Froud of the goblins who then inhabited the world, and of the Labyrinth—that great defensive structure built by one of the goblin kings to protect his subjects from the advance of the ungoblin world. He told how the goblins retreated farther and farther into the Labyrinth until it became the only place they could inhabit, in the tearful times after the Great Collapse of Good Governance.* But, more importantly, he led Froud across the Crater to the Olduvai Gorge itself, and there, from a deep crack in the basalt, he pulled out an old, old chest. When the Old Barman of the Ngorongoro Hilton finally managed to open the chest, Froud saw, to his amazement, that it contained no less than forty-three dusty, mouldering notebooks—the exact number of cases of Chevalier-Montrachet he had left!** To his even greater astonishment, each notebook proved to be packed with sketches and lightning portraits of all the goblins who inhabited the Labyrinth in those long vanished times.

Froud instantly gave up *piscepodiatry* (which wasn't all that hard to do) and devoted the rest of his sober moments to studying this cornucopia of ancient goblin portraiture.

The goblin artist whose work had been so miraculously preserved appears to have been a certain Dåshe.† His technique was quick and direct, but unfortunately his concentration was less than satisfactory, and many of the "portraits" consisted of but a few lines thrown down apparently randomly on the page. However, after years of study and hardly any flower-arranging, Froud was able to compare and cross-reference the lines and fragments so as to build up fuller likenesses of the goblins portrayed. At length (i.e., 70 cases of Savigny-Lés-Beaune, 12 Ladoix, 46 Nuits-St-Georges, 27 Romanée-Conti, 65 Vosne-Romanée, 54 Chabolle-Musigny and 435 Chablis) Froud was even able to reconstruct their names.

This book is the result of all that wine and study, and represents the fullest record yet discovered of the Goblins of the Labyrinth.

* *The Great Collapse of Good Governance*: See the entry for Bübl, page 18.

**Perhaps the greatest mystery surrounding this whole story is how Froud was able to ship such vast quantities of fine French wines into the Serengeti Plain.

†*Dåshe*: For his self-portrait see plate 56.

Qüiver

The Tale of Qüiver

The tale of Qüiver is popular amongst the humbler goblins—and especially amongst those who are not yet qualified to "shoot from memory." The tale goes something like this.

It was the Eve of All Owls' Night, when traditionally the Goblin Army harvests its own karbobs* and roasts them around the great well of the castle, before retiring to the North West Tower to drain the traditional Tun of Owl Wine.† A small goblin named Qüiver was detailed for guard duty. Now Qüiver was a very inexperienced goblin who had not yet been instructed in the use of the bone crossbow nor, of course, "shooting from memory."

Well, he stood there for several hours, listening to the sounds of merrymaking coming from the courtyard. He could hear the crackle of the great fire and smell the roasting karbobs, and he began to feel very sorry for himself and very hungry. He kept on feeling his own karbobs (he had one under his left armpit and another just inside his groin), and he sighed because he knew that by the next day they might have burst into leaf and it would be too late. As he was thinking these sad thoughts, he was startled by a strange noise coming out of the darkness. Thinking it might be a Short Enemy (the only kind he was allowed to challenge), he raised his bone crossbow and squeaked: "Halt and all that!" (the traditional goblin challenge). But the creature-in-the-night merely made more noises and started calling out names and being extremely unsympathetic. Now an experienced goblin would have ignored all this, but Qüiver put his bone crossbow to his shoulder and fired. Unfortunately, a goblin who has not been instructed in the art of "shooting from memory" should never, ever fire in the pitch darkness. Nor, of course, should he put his bone crossbow to his shoulder the wrong way round. However, this is just what Qüiver did. Consequently the bone bolt shot straight back towards the castle, entered the window of the North West Tower, and pierced the traditional Tun of Owl Wine.

**Karbobs (Karbobus karbobis)*: Small tubers that flourish in the warm, wet cracks and crannies under armour. The tuber must be eaten when it has sprouted but before it has begun to flower; otherwise, it can be extremely dangerous.

†Owl Wine is prepared from carefully pressed owls, fermented and kept for many years in oak barrels. It is not particularly nice.

The creature-in-the-night, of course, could see all this and collapsed in laughter—much to the bewilderment of little Qüiver.

Meanwhile, the Owl Wine began to spray out of the barrel and out of the window of the North West Tower, forming a fine rain that descended down onto the merry courtyard below. The Owl-Wine rain got heavier and heavier, until it put out the bonfires where the karbobs were still only half-roasted and drove the other goblins back inside. Disappointed by the frustration of their feast, they retired to the North West Tower to drown their sorrows. But when they got there, of course, they discovered the Great Tun empty and the canapés‡ all sodden.

The whole feast was abandoned and set up for the day after All Owls' Night. When Qüiver came off guard duty and learnt what had happened, he was so embarrassed that he harvested his own karbobs there and then, roasted them, and sent them to the Lord High Goblin's daughter. She was so touched by this heroic act of self-sacrifice that she declared that the karbob feast should ever fall on the day *after* All Owls' Night. And so it is still celebrated to this day .

‡Not canapés as we understand them, of course. Goblin canapés consist of such things as wood sandwiches, live bird soup, and "string" ("string" is a worm dish invented for All Owls' Night Eve by Eled the Worm-Trainer [see plate 23], who had a lot of pensioned-off and disabled worms to get rid of).

QÜI
VER
leather cowl
2 of these
Fig 3
Fig 1
1
2
3
4
5

LUERK

Luerk

The Story of Luerk

The story of Luerk is a very sad one. In fact, it is *so* sad ... so unutterably pitiable and unenduringly misery-making that it is never told. Indeed the last time it *was* told was several hundred and fifty goblin years ago, when it was told to a small goblin named Hattersley,* who immediately went into a melancholic decline from which he never recovered. After the small goblin's demise from this surfeit of grief, the story of Luerk was banned altogether from the Tale-Tellers' Circuit, and the last goblin bard who knew it died long ago. Hence it is (perhaps fortunately) impossible to reconstruct the unhappy history. Only amongst the descendants of Luerk do snippets of the original tale survive to bear witness to its apotheosis of lachrymosity. There are hints of a fatal laundry bill (which, some say, remains unpaid to this day), suggestions of rust in the armour and heart, and occasionally you will hear dark mutterings about a beautiful visitor from the ungoblin world named Brassica Oleracea Botrytis, with whom the youthful Luerk fell head over heels in love, only to return home one day to learn that his mother had made her into a cauliflower cheese.

The significance of the small chiming apparatus, apparent in all representations of Luerk, is uncertain. Some believe it may have been a way of communicating with the laundry company to check on items that had gone astray .

**Hattersley*: This is, of course, an odd name for a goblin, but it is believed to have derived from his mother, who found it embroidered on a name tag affixed to the towelling diapers of a changeling brought back from the ungoblin world in the times long since remembered.

Bakarbobs Karnobissica

(Fig. 4 and Fig. 5)

Distantly related to the karbob family (see the *Tale of Qüiver*, page 12) these tubers grow only behind the ears and around the necks of the much maligned Tallow Goblins (figs. h, b, and c). The Tallow Goblins are much maligned primarily because they are disgusting, shifty, aggressive little freaks who would cut their own granny open, stuff her, and use her as a sofa as soon as look at her. In fact, a sofa made out of their granny is considered an essential piece of furniture for all Tallow Goblin households.

The Tallow Goblins grow the bakarbobs as offensive weapons. Harvested when they get to the size of the Tallow Goblin's own head, they are gutted (in much the same way as the grannies), the contents eaten by the Tallow Goblin (I told you they were disgusting), and the skin of the tuber sewn up to form a handbag. All the Tallow Goblins' non-earthly possessions (including the granny-sofa) are crushed up into a ball and placed in the bakarbob handbag, which is then swung with considerable force at anything or anyone that comes within spitting distance—and Tallow Goblins can spit up to distances of over half a mile!

PLATE 3

Bübl

Originally destined for a job in the Servile Service, Bübl became unemployed about the time of the Great Collapse of Good Governance in the Labyrinth.* He took a job creating noses for noseless goblins (see figs. s, m, t, y, and 4), but without a great deal of success (see figs. s, m, t, y, and 4). Bübl was forced to eke out a living by hiring himself out as a can opener, but, even in this humble role, his career appeared to be blighted by the total absence in the Labyrinth of tinned comestibles.

**The Great Collapse of Good Governance in the Labyrinth*: The real truth is now lost in the mists of memory, but it is fabled that the Labyrinth was once ruled with Wisdom, Joy, Order, and Hope. The goblin rulers were modest, self-effacing creatures, whose only desire was to promote the happiness and well-being of their fellows, and—more importantly—to be forgotten for so doing. In fact, every goblin who took a post in the Goblin Government had to take an Oath of Anonymity so that nothing he did should be done for the purpose of preserving his name for posterity. The Great Collapse of Good Governance occurred when the Oath of Anonymity began to be abused, and goblin rulers began to assume pseudonyms that they became just as vain about and eager to have remembered as if they were their real names.

The other great safeguard in the Times of Good Governance was that no goblin ruler had any power whatsoever. All they could do was suggest ideas, and the good ideas were then adopted by general consent. Once the goblin rulers started to force others to do as they wanted, the writing was on the wall—at least as far as Good Governance was concerned.

Sqeek

Able to signal messages as far as the eye can see, Sqeek (or Semaphorus Quickius Easius Elasticus Komfortabilis, to give him his full name) is as unreliable a goblin as any you are unlikely to meet in the Labyrinth. His innate propensity to introduce scatalogical references into even the simplest message has caused shame and self-reproach to all who have availed themselves of his telegraphic services.

BÜBAL
A
B
SQEEK

The Serpent Sword of Elmerillion

(Fig. 1)

The Serpent Sword of Elmerillion has been fabled in Goblin Folklore and Tales ever since it was first fabled in them.

It was forged by the Great Elf—the Blacksmith Elf—the Maker-of-Nails—the White Wizard of the Elfin Mire—who gave it as his only weapon to Loph, the Garter Goblin, to fight his duel with Isk, the Grey-Legged Wanderer from the Murks of Thell. The Serpent Sword of Elmerillion proved its worth at once in that dreadful encounter, and ever after it has come to be a goblin byword for absolute uselessness. Loph was killed instantly, before he could even lift the cumbersome Serpent Sword, and Isk, the Grey-Legged Wanderer, turned on his heel and wandered back to the Murks of Thell, laughing to himself and eating slices of Grit Cake (see fig. t). The Great Elf—the Blacksmith Elf—the Maker-of-Nails—the White Wizard of the Elfin Mire—never made another sword after that, and the Serpent Sword of Elmerillion was hung in the Great Hall of Unconventional and Useless Objects, in between the Giant Hairy Pin and the Unwarmable Rat-Tickling Device.

Grit Cake (one slice)

(Fig. t)

A favourite goblin delicacy. The hard core and rubble that forms the bulk of the cake mix is separated out in the goblin digestive system and stored in the upper part of the back, producing a hump of great weight, which inevitably produces the bent and crouching posture that goblins find irresistibly attractive—as demonstrated by the unnamed goblin maiden in the illustration.

When toasted on the halberd (fig. b), grit cake is turned into a useful roofing material, which can also be served cold under scrambled frogs' eggs.

Püg

Püg (pronounced, for no apparent reason, "guppie") was hailed by many as the greatest artist of his generation. His early canvases—such as *The Death and Destruction of a Million Goblins of Uncertain Dispositions* or his widely acclaimed *Heads Being Banged by Something Big and Horrible*—were wildly popular amongst goblins of all types and dimensions. His popularity began to wane, however, as he moved onto more experimental and—to the goblin mind—more controversial subjects, such as *Several Beautiful Princesses Enjoying a Wonderful Picnic Under the Most Pleasant Circumstances* or the much reviled *Happy Goblins Being Pleasant to Someone Who Was Kind to Them*.

As his work fell into disfavour Püg (still pronounced "guppie") became personally more cantankerous and irascible. It was not, however, until after the howl of critical derision provoked by his *A Bunch of Nice Flowers* that he finally sank into hopeless iracundity and began the series of armed assaults on critics and public alike, with which his name has become synonymous. Goblins of all dimensions and types still refer to such behaviour as "guppienacity."

Fig 1
Fig t
Püg
Fig 12
f

Fig 34c
PILCH
FØD
DER
Fig 9 of Fig 13

Pilch

Of all goblins in the whole Labyrinth it is the goblins who bear the name of Pilch that have the strangest life cycle.

They each start out as an aquatic larva (see fig. 34c) swimming aimlessly through the Great Seas of Silence along the Ruined Shore. After several years of this, without any apparent change or growth, the larvae are then eaten by the Badder Fish (see fig. 34d), which then—after approximately 3²⁄₃₁ minutes—explodes, releasing vast hordes of miniature goblins all bearing the name of Pilch.

Unfortunately (or, perhaps, fortunately) the tiny Pilch goblins cannot swim, and so they all drown. However, on very rare occasions, a Badder Fish has been caught and brought to the surface in the 3²⁄₃₁ of a second after it has consumed some Pilch larvae, and it has then exploded on land. The resulting tidal wave of goblins (all bearing the name of Pilch), which has swept through the Labyrinth, is regarded as one of the worst disasters known to the goblin world, since everyone knows that all goblins who bear the name of Pilch are the most boring table companions it is ever possible to meet.

Fødder

Little is known about this goblin beyond its dual role as an offensive weapon and teapot.

Fødder was last seen in active service during the Great War to Liberate Horseshoes (see fig. 9). The war lasted several hundred years and in the end proved inconclusive.

Horseshoes continue to be trodden underfoot by horses of all social backgrounds and shades of opinions (of which horses tend to not have many). And the result was considered irrelevant, anyway, as, by the end of the Great War to Liberate Horseshoes, nobody could remember who had started it in the first place, which side they were fighting, or why it mattered.

Pöngö

Nothing whatsoever is known about this goblin.

Skøåt

Skøåt, the Royal Nail Clipper, wanders through the Labyrinth with his assistant, Lilac, clipping the toenails and fingernails of all goblins unlucky enough to get in his way. "If only they'd give us tools more suited to the job, there'd be fewer toes and fingers lost ..." is his constant complaint. Nevertheless, he persists in plying his bloody trade, with halberd and poleaxe, wherever and whenever he can. "Stick out your toes!" is his cry. "Fingers akimbo!"

Some say that Skøåt is the sole reason why there are so many three-toed, unfingered goblins in the Labyrinth ... others blame it all on Lilac.

PÖN GÖ

SKØ ÅT
Fig 3c

Böing

Feared by goblin maidens through the centuries, Racing Goblins (such as Böing) are remarkable (to say the least!) for their detachable members (see fig. V xii). These members are invariably kept in small (or sometimes large) pouches and left lying around on benches, sent through the post, or secreted under bushes. The members are capable of operating totally independently of the Racing Goblin himself and have been responsible for some of the most ill-judged unions in the history of the Labyrinth.

BÖI NG
III vi
Fig V xii
A
D
Fig 8b
Fig 8c

Sneek & Sküell

Two of the most evil-hearted villains you are likely to come across in the Labyrinth, Sneek and Sküell, lived as bandits for many years on the edge of the Great Howling Gulf. Why they chose this particular spot, where hardly any goblins ever venture, is uncertain, but they were both notorious for what they *would* have done if there had been anyone to do it to. For example, it is rumoured that Sneek would have disguised himself as an easygoing polo player, who would challenge innocent passers-by to a game of polo which almost certainly would always end in his winning. Sküell (see art on following page), on the other hand, would have lain in wait for travellers and wandering folk, and then waited for them to have a picnic, and as soon as they'd eaten and drunk too much (which goblins always do) he would have leapt out on them and stolen their toothpicks! As I say, they are a black-hearted pair.

Their careers of putative outrage and evil were eventually brought to an end by the great goblin detective Dogsthörpe (see plate 35).

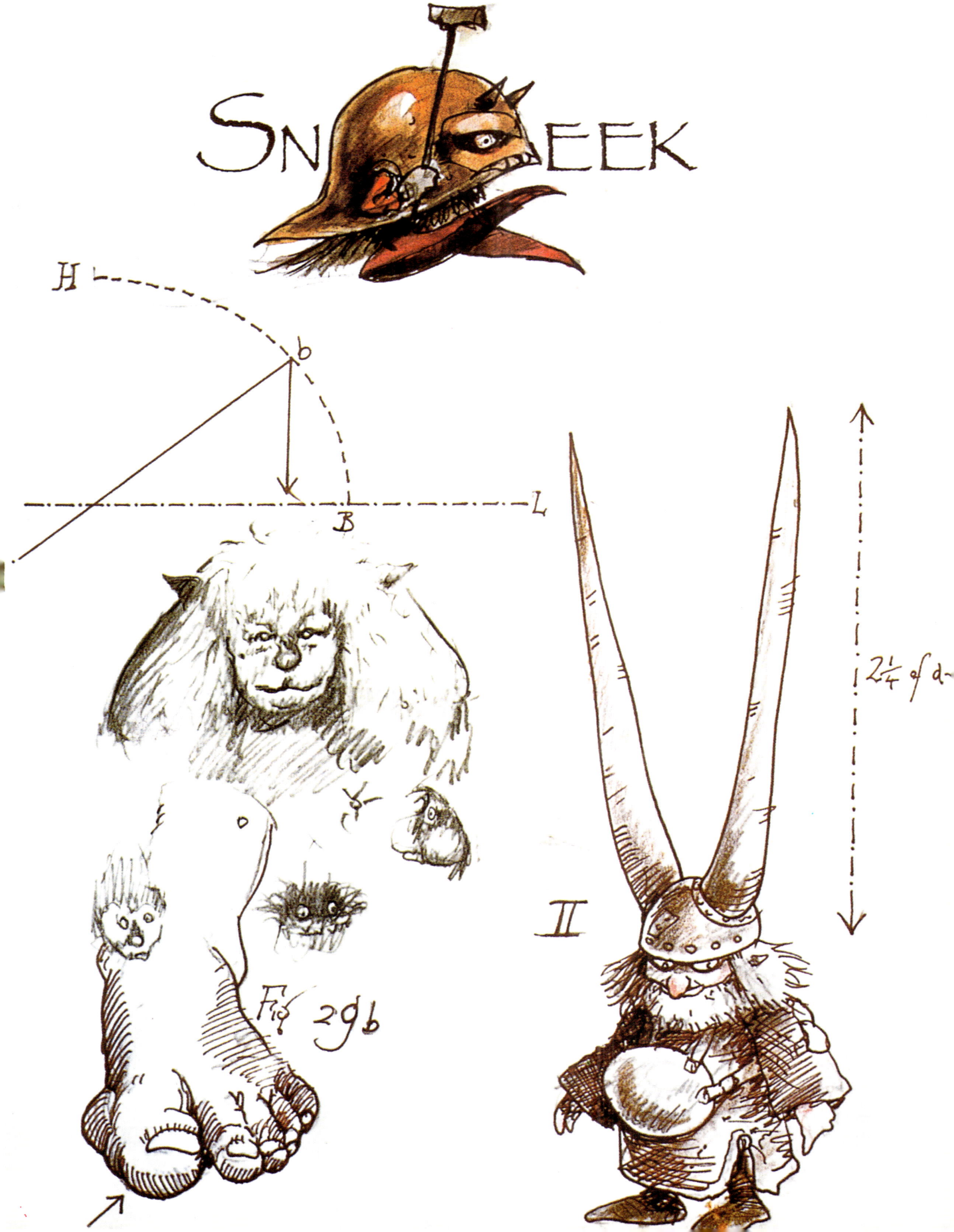
SN EEK
H
b
L
B
Fig 29b
II
2¼ of a-

SKÜE LL
3
a
f
I
II

CÄNDLE WÍC

Cändlewic

One of the Keepers of the Goblin Hoard (see Låmpsöniüs, page 84, and Agmøür, page 103).

Zĩtzĩe

Unexpectedly renowned as the most beautiful of all goblins, Zĩtzĩe is nevertheless also the most feared. It is the contents of her handbag that create panic and despondency wherever she goes shopping. For in her handbag she secretes a selection of the most evil and barbarous weapons devised by the goblin mind (see fig. p through z to qf). For instance: the Short Hope Knife (x) can cut through even the most optimistic goblin's highest aspirations in a matter of seconds. Similarly the Dream-Pick (qf) can puncture the most wonderful and rapturous reveries, whilst the fiendish Angst-Plug (f)—if driven in firmly—can bottle up a goblin's fears until the hapless creature explodes in an outburst of acute diffidence. Perhaps, however, it is the Luck-Ladle (fig. 371d) that is most feared by all goblins great and small. With a single scoop of the ladle, Zĩtzĩe is capable of creaming off an entire lifetime of good fortune from any unfortunate goblin.

Zĩtzĩe, however, does bake the most scrumptious worzel flapjacks.

ZITZIE
Rear Armour
Mail
Dishcloth
Fig 371

Gibbergeist

In the grand tradition of goblin tragedians and tripe-buglers, Gibbergeist has performed in every goblin theatre this side of the Terrible Howling Gulf. His interpretations of such classic goblin tragic heroes as King Fear and that bleakest of all tragic figures—the Wobbling Window Cleaner—are legendary. So too is his ability to create a major role out of almost nothing. It is rumoured, for example, that in the part of Second Soldier from the Right in the Back Row he once reduced an entire theatre to helpless tears by his long and protracted death, which took over three hours—and *then* half a day of encores. Perhaps his most famous performance, however, was as the Ghost of Breakfasts Past in *The Last Prawn*—a 150-hour epic set in a self-service mortuary and much beloved by goblins. It was in this role that Gibbergeist first entertained his audience on the tripe bugle (fig. x). Gibbergeist is also famous as the defeater of Börgis Khån (see page 99).

GIBBER GEIST
Fig x

Amâm Pherrüginüs

Heavily armed birds are, of course, always a menace, but the Amâm is particularly so since it is an extremely bad flier. It is by no means uncommon for the Amâm to fall out of the sky in mid-flight—sometimes because its wings have stuck together,* sometimes simply because it is *too* heavily armed. But whatever the reason, an armed Amâm falling out of the sky, emitting its characteristic curse of "Damn you, Gravity!" is a terrifying and often fatal memory for anyone who has experienced it.

*The Amâm is peculiar amongst the feathered species in that it has no feathers—only hairs—and is thus obliged to filch feathery substances from wheresoever it can and stick them onto itself with crab and eel glue. Thus the Amâm is not only very heavy and clumsy but also extremely smelly.

Amåm Pherrüginüs

Tr̂ysöp

Under Tr̂ysöp's shabby, unfriendly exterior beats an even shabbier and unfriendlier heart. Tr̂ysöp's heart, however, is one of the most remarkable of all phenomena in the whole Labyrinth. For a start, it is located on his back (fig. 2). In the second place, Tr̂ysöp's heart is equipped with legs (fig. 2) and is capable of wandering off for long periods of time. When goblins refer to Tr̂ysöp as being "a heartless karbob-snatcher"* they often mean it literally. Exactly what Tr̂ysöp's heart does when it climbs down off his back and wanders away, no one is quite certain. It has been followed as far as the Gaming Dens of Weiss, and it is rumoured to have been seen on an adventure holiday amongst the Dental Remains of Plaque. But no one has been able to confirm either sighting, and many goblins believe it simply goes somewhere quiet for a nice rest and a lie down.

When heartless, Tr̂ysöp becomes surprisingly tractable and charming. He displays a tendency to give sweets to old ladies and helps fit young children across the street. But when his heart is in place, he is a fiendish monster, obsessed with consuming vast quantities of karbobs.

*For karbobs, see the *Tale of Qüiver* (page 12).

TRŶ SÖP
Fig 3
Fig 2
Gauntlet
Fig 3
Fig 2

Frölöw

The goblin game of Lunchball is played wherever goblins gather enough spotted jumpers (fig. b) together to form two teams. And as each team consists of (at least) 2361 goblins, it isn't often that they can gather together enough spotted jumpers to play! The game itself is fast and furious, although complicated by the fact that both sides are dressed identically. The object of the game is to *eat* the ball, and (as you can imagine) with 4722 ravenous goblins loose, this happens within the first few seconds. The rest of the game is spent trying to find out which goblins actually managed to eat the ball and how ill they feel.

One of the all-time greatest Lunchball players was, of course, Frölöw, who succeeded in consuming the entire ball himself on no less than thirteen consecutive occasions. This is no mean feat as the ball is six feet in diameter and made of solid teak (fig. c).

Fåüstüs

Another sportsman, Fåüstüs, is renowned as an exponent of that most dangerous of all sports—Goblin Head-Banging.

The sharp horns are tipped with a uniquely unpleasant poison, which enters the victim's blood system and, within twenty-four hours, makes his trousers drop off.

The Goblin Head-Banging Finals are feared for months beforehand, and many attempts have been made to ban the sport altogether. However, the Goblin Head-Banging Authority is a powerful vested interest that has lobbied successfully to keep the sport going for over two thousand years. They argue that if the sport were banned, potential Goblin Head-Bangers would turn to something even more dangerous—like knitting.*

*For knitting, see page 44.

FRÖL
ÖV
Visor
Cowl
Knee
FÅÜ
STÜS
goggles
stud

Goblin Knitting

An extremely dangerous and foolhardy exercise, goblin knitting is undertaken with only one knitting needle—but one that is barbed and has two razor-sharp edges to it. It takes *two* goblins to knit a scarf or a sweater and demands a remarkable degree of coordination and cooperation, which is, quite honestly, totally alien to the goblin nature. Hence the knitting usually breaks down into a violent argument, and blood flows within a matter of one or two stitches. In fact, nowadays the traditional preliminaries of carding and skeining the wool, discussing the knitting pattern and choosing a pretty colour, are usually dispensed with, and the knitters get straight down to the business of hacking each other to pieces.

Extinct Mammal

The small mammal pictured at the bottom of plate 18 is actually extinct, although no one has yet had the heart to tell it. It still lives amongst the Rubbish Mounds of Yore and eats anything that can answer the three simple questions it puts to it. A curious beast.

Blue

PLATE 19

The Sacred Bone of Whence

(Fig. Vii)

One of the most revered relics in the Labyrinth, this ancient bone rests in the Silent Sepulchre on the Holy Hill. From time immemorial, goblins have made the great pilgrimage across the Wastes of Wandering, over the Great Dust Desert, and into the Mysterious Mountains to seek it out and pay their respects. Great healing powers are attributed to the relic. For example, it is said that those who touch the Holy Knob (fig. A) will receive a large reward in the post. Those who kiss the sacred spots (figs. D and T) will gain relief from anything that irritates them on a Thursday. Pilgrims who simply point at the Blessed "I" will acquire the gift of making great sandwiches, whilst those who press their noses on the Venerable "E" will be granted the gift of Eternal Indifference (if they want it).

The only worry about all this for most goblins is that the relic is *so* old that no one is quite sure what it is a relic of. Suggestions are consequently left in a little box beside the Silent Sepulchre, and every year the box is opened up and the contents ceremoniously thrown away.

A
Fig VII
Fig 14

Bec & Cäül

The Labyrinth has produced surprisingly few philosophers of any note. Perhaps the best known was the Wise One of the Plains, whose chief contribution to Knowledge was the theory that the length of time spent thinking about any one subject was in *inverse proportion* to the number of eggs you could eat. The philosopher Bec later elaborated this theory by pointing out that the number of eggs you could eat varied according to the size of each egg, and that a Twark's egg (for Twark, see page 54) was *much* smaller than the egg of the Klutton (see fig. 129d on page 81). However, it was not until another great goblin thinker by the name of Cäül developed both ideas that the pattern of Goblin Philosophy was set for future generations. Cäül pointed out that neither the Twark's egg nor the Klutton's egg are particularly nice to eat (the Twark's egg tastes of corduroy trousers while the Klutton's has more of a worsted flavour). Thus it could be induced that thinking about *anything* for *any period* was a complete waste of time. This theory became immediately popular with all goblins, and Bec and Cäül were able to devote their declining years to knitting (see page 44) and harassing the small extinct mammal pictured on page 46.

A Target Goblin

(Fig. H)

Goblins like this are used as targets during military exercises in the Labyrinth. It is a thankless and nerve-racking job. Fig. 10 gives some idea of how such goblins feel after a day's work.

Bec & Cäül

Hörtenz

The Great Plain of Hair was subject to frequent flooding. Even a single drop of rain would produce a flash flood of drastic proportions.

The goblins who lived on the Great Plain of Hair therefore had to adapt to a way of life in which instant deluge and instant drought were a regular everyday happening. They did this by wearing shoes that could double up as boats, as well as cloaks that could also serve as sails. In this way, the constant inundations did not disturb the fabric of everyday life. Indeed, the goblins of the Great Plain of Hair became so inured to the persistent alternations between flood and aridity that they began to scarcely notice the difference anymore. And thus it became imperative to employ Hörtenz, the Water-Dipper, whose job it was to wander about the Great Plain of Hair, measuring the height of the flood with his measuring stick and calling out the depths. He would warn the goblins of the Plain, for example, not to sunbathe when the waters stood at level f, or not to do handstands until the waters had subsided down to level bII. Hörtenz's voice would ring out continually across the Great Plain of Hair and the Flood Water: "No marble playing today!" or "All is dry! All is dry! No high diving, deep sea trawling, or underwater gym today!"

HÖRTENZ
siii
iv
h
g
f
I
a
b
c
bII
Fig IV
Fig 9

PLATE 22

The Twark

The Twark (small figure on right) is a small rodent remarkable for two things. In the first place it lays an extremely small egg (see Bec and Cäül, page 50). The egg is so small that it cannot be seen with the naked eye. Indeed it cannot be seen with a magnifying glass—or even with an electron microscope. It is, in fact, the smallest particle known to science—*so* small that some scientists even doubt whether it exists at all. Nevertheless, the Twark goes on happily making its nests and laying its eggs as it always has done, and as if everybody could see them and had absolutely no doubts about whether they existed or not. And perhaps the Twark is right, for no matter what they may think about the Twark's egg's lack of physical presence, *all* goblins agree that it smells and tastes of corduroy trousers. For the famous poem "Ode to a Twark's Egg" by the poet Brêgg, see page 79.

The second remarkable thing about the Twark is that it washes itself on the inside but not on the outside. It is, consequently, an extremely smelly animal, but a great kisser.

Eled the Worm-Tamer

Eled the Worm-Tamer vowed to be rich.
He climbed up a mountain that stood in a ditch.
When he got to the summit, all he could see
Was the top of the ditch, the Worm Michael, and me.

Thus sing all small goblins on their first day at school. Like so many nursery rhymes, the meaning of "Eled the Worm-Tamer" is elusive.

How can a mountain "stand in a ditch"? Who or what is the "Worm Michael"? Who is the "me" of the rhyme? And yet there seems to be some factual basis behind the ditty, since there was a goblin in antiquity known as Eled the Worm-*Trainer*. The historical Eled ran a Worm Circus in the High and Mighty Days of the Empire of the Labyrinth. There are descriptions still extant of some of the displays and events that took place in Eled's Worm Circus. One account, for example, records how sixty worms balanced end-to-end to form a teetering tower of worms, the top of which disappeared into the clouds. On another occasion, Eled himself battled a huge sixty-foot-long worm with razor-sharp teeth, who could put its victims to sleep by reciting long elegiac poems. And in yet another display, Eled trained six worms to think logically. This last was, perhaps, his greatest achievement as a worm-trainer, but it was also his last, since it proved extremely unpopular with the other goblins. What happened was this. Once the worms could think logically, they said to themselves: "Why should we do all the work (thinking), while Eled takes all the profit and just gives us worm food? Let us strike for a percentage of the profits. With this percentage (which we won't spend, since worm food is dirt cheap) we will hire the services of vast hordes of huge sixty-foot-long worms with razor-sharp teeth, who can recite elegiac poetry, to form an army with which we can smash our goblin oppressors forever! Then we shall build a Golden New World, where worms can be free—free to live their lives in peace and plenty—free to live and love as only worms can in the secure joys of wormhood and wormliness, reaching ever onwards, ever outwards towards a better future and the ultimate happiness of worm domination! Wriggle! It's so exciting! Let's eat some more dirt!"

Fortunately for the goblins, this plan never reached fruition, because the prospects so dazzled the worms' minds that they lost their powers of reason and started trying to lift heavy metal objects, which inevitably squashed them all. It was, however, a narrow squeak, and Eled the Worm-Trainer was ruined. He spent his declining years bashing a small worm named Mitchell over the head with a spiked mace (see fig. 72).

B

53
SPÜE

Spüe

One form of Flying Goblin that nests in great numbers under the eaves of most public buildings in the Labyrinth, the Spüe are remarkable for being able to inflict a really severe bite. The effects of the bite vary from goblin to goblin. Some goblins, when bitten, develop a nasty rash that matures, festers, and turns into a huge fungus that is considered to be a culinary delicacy (rather like truffles). Culling the fungus, however, is extremely painful, sometimes fatal, and goblins bitten by the Spüe naturally tend to try to conceal their condition. Not all goblins bitten by the Spüe, however, develop this rash. Some develop hitherto unsuspected musical talents and are able to give virtuoso performances on any known instrument. Others develop knee growths that enable them to stand at odd angles. As I say, you never know quite what will happen when you're bitten by a Spüe.

Gürtie

The same (see Spüe, above) is *not* true, however, of Gürtie bites—the effects of which are invariably nasty, fatal, and quick. Fortunately, on the other hand, the Gürtie themselves are not particularly aggressive. They are prone to swoop down on you and make you a nice mug of hot cocoa. Sometimes they will steal up on one from behind with platefuls of sandwiches and canapés.* At other times they will simply force their victims to enjoy life a little more.

The tail of the Gürtie is remarkable for having three ends to it (figs. 90, 6, and 201).

* For canapés, see the *Tale of Qüiver*, page 12.

GÜRTIE

PLATE 26

Agnes

Agnes is one of the many scavenging goblins that inhabit the Wide Tract of Rottenness that was formed after the Great Collapse of Good Governance in the Labyrinth (see note on Bübl, page 18).

Agnes is capable of collecting and carrying seventy times her own weight in discarded economic theories and abandoned political objectives. The empty promises, hollow opinions, and worthless public statements that litter the Wide Tract are all snapped up by this voracious creature. She then delivers them to Gürdy the Burnisher (see page 66), who polishes them up as good as new, if not better, and resells them to the ambitious and unscrupulous of all ages.

AG
NES

Hywr & Löwr

It is a little-known fact that reproduction amongst goblins is strictly forbidden by ancient laws dating back to the Great Collapse of Good Governance in the Labyrinth (see notes on Bübl, page 18, and Agnes, page 62). How or why such a law came to be enacted is still far from clear, but it is typical of the sort of legislation that was being passed at the time of the Great Collapse.* Needless to say, reproduction amongst goblins carries on unabated in the time-honoured tradition, but the two Inspectors of Reproduction, Hywr and his aide, Löwr, are forever on the alert to pinpoint possible infringements of the law.

The act of generation amongst goblins is unique in that it creates an extremely powerful odour, which is detectable up to distances of several miles. Thus the Inspectors of Reproduction are equipped with special scent-detection apparatus, which can pinpoint the source and range of any reproductive odours. Unfortunately the sensitivity of the equipment is such (and the proclivity of goblins for reproduction such) that, once they have donned the scent-detection equipment, the inspectors are overwhelmed with constant odours from all directions and at all times. They become virtually paralyzed, unable to move in any one direction more than another, and—eventually—succumb to the same generative instincts that they are meant to suppress. They become, to put it plainly, sex-mad maniacs, and are forced to turn themselves in for Contemplated Reproduction.

Reform of this bizarre law is constantly being canvassed, but unfortunately the Reproductive De-Odorant Industry is so powerful (despite the fact that their product is patently useless) that no amendment of the law has been achieved in two thousand years of heated debate.

*Other laws of this era are: The Law Against Holding Up Any Kind of Lunch Box, The Anti-Smirking Laws, The Prevention of Thoughtful Pauses Act, and the Abolition of Death (1896) Act.

HYWR
bi
bii
biv
bvii
IV
b
d
LÖWR
Fig 1
Fig 2

Røem Bååbå

The Goblin Prime Minister since the Great Collapse of Good Governance in the Labyrinth (see notes above to Bübl, page 18, Agnes, page 62, and Hywr and Löwr, page 64), Røem Bååbå is, curiously, greatly loved and admired by the great majority of goblins. Røem Bååbå's aptitude for administration is, of course, negligible, his sense of justice and fair play naturally non-existent, his powers of organization and delegation hardly worth talking about, and his authority, as you would expect, a standing joke. But even greater than all these other virtues (to the goblin mind) is the fact that he is inhabited by the World's Biggest Flea (fig. 45d). Once, or sometimes twice, a day the World's Biggest Flea will leap off the Prime Minister and hop around the room to the great delight of all goblins with an interest in politics. Any goblin who is fortunate enough to be leapt over by the flea receives an endowment from the Prime Minister equivalent to the amount of gold that can be stuffed into his right nostril. However, should the flea happen to bump into any goblin, the goblin is declared to have infringed the Prime Minister's Hair Space and is immediately executed. (Although, of course, within the terms of the Abolition of Death [1896] Act, "execution" means being forced to lie in bed all day if it's raining and you've got a snuffle that makes you feel a bit under the weather.) The flea's name, by the way, is Betsy.

Gürdy

For Gürdy the Burnisher, see note to Agnes, page 62.

RØEM BÅÅBÅ
Fig I
Fig 5
Fig 45a.

GÜRDY

Qüilk

No goblin marriage ceremony would be complete without the services of Qüilk. During the ceremony the Happy Couple of Dozen* hang out their hearts (see fig. 3c) on the ceremonial Fishstick, and Qüilk then stands on duty for the duration of the dancing and nibbling.† At an appointed hour (or whenever Qüilk happens to think of the word "lump-like"), he lowers the Fishstick and announces that the marriage is at an end. The brides and grooms are duly pronounced divorced and everyone breathes a sigh of relief. They then retrieve their hearts and retire to the Refreshment Field to grub up the traditional Yuk Roots (fig. 3f) that are then partly eaten straight out of the ground. Then everyone goes "Yuk!" and throws them at Qüilk.

*Goblin marriages are always between at least twenty-four goblins in any combination of sexes.

†*Nibbling:* During the goblin wedding ceremony, the Happy Couple of Dozen dance around a sort of maypole, which is supposed to symbolize the hairdressers who were the first goblins to get married. They then each in turn nibble a bit of fish or else do some carpentry. The tendency nowadays is increasingly to concentrate on the carpentry part of the ceremony—sometimes extending it to a bit of bricklaying, concrete-mixing, the erection of scaffolding and general labouring—so that most modern goblin weddings are indistinguishable from a construction site. Such weddings, however, are regarded as infinitely more practical than the older style.

QÜIST
QÜIRK
QÜÅRK
QÜILK
Fig 3f
Fig 3c

Aprön

Aprön is one of the best-loved juve-leads in the goblin theatrical world. Attractive to male and female goblins alike, Aprön is, in fact, the nearest thing to a heartthrob that can be found in the Labyrinth.

He (or "she," according to taste) performs on the great feast days, such as Toe-Feast Night or All Owls' Night (see notes to Qüiver, page 12 and Mæliciöüs, page 74) when he/she will also give virtuoso performances of the favourite goblin classics such as *The Play About a Goblin Who Fell into a Bucket of Something or Other and Then Oh! What Happened Next I Can't Remember but You Know the Piece Because It's So Famous Everybody Knows It.*

Aprön is also a master of disguise. With nothing more than a pan, four of these, three of these, a dishcloth, ducks' feet, a tin of peas, seventy pork chops, some sugar, and some gherkins, he/she can make herself/himself look like ... well ... nothing in particular, but goblins always seem to be impressed by it for some reason.

Aprön has also made many hit singles, although no one has ever heard any of them.

pan
4 of these
3 of these
APRÖN
Dishcloth
Duck feet
Tin of Peas
Pork Chops (70
Sugar
Ghèrkins

Mæliciöüs

Despite his appearance, Mæliciöüs *(Mæliciöüs Mælificiosus)* is actually one of the most dependable and useful of goblins. In part this is due to his placid and benign nature, but more importantly it is due to the fact that he is entirely *empty*. His main use lies in his wandering around battlefields or other scenes of carnage (such as Toe-Feast Night* or the Night of Ten Thousand Joys†). When the Cleaning Goblins step on his toe, the top of his helmet flips back, enabling them to jettison the detritus of war into him.

No one knows what becomes of this rubbish, but suffice it to say that no one has ever been invited back to his place!

*See page 72 and below.

†See below.

Fig. 104

Despite its appearance, this is *not* an offensive weapon. It is, in fact, a bottle of Gnolfurgis Wine. This wine is chiefly drunk on occasions such as Toe-Feast Night or the Night of Ten Thousand Joys,‡ when thousands of such bottles are consumed. The Gnolfurgis Wine bottle developed because goblins generally experienced great difficulty in drawing corks from conventional bottles. To the goblin mind, simply pulling a cork out of a bottle seemed a bit of an anticlimax. The Gnolfurgis bottle, on the other hand, is opened by racking it up to the required angle and lighting the fuse. A large explosive device in the neck of the bottle sends the well-sharpened stopper several hundred yards at a considerable velocity.

As you can imagine, the consumption of Gnolfurgis Wine is inevitably accompanied by tremendous casualties—mainly owing to the highly toxic nature of the wine itself. Half a glassful being fatal for most smaller goblins.

‡See previous entry.

iv
6
MÆL ÍCÍÖÜS

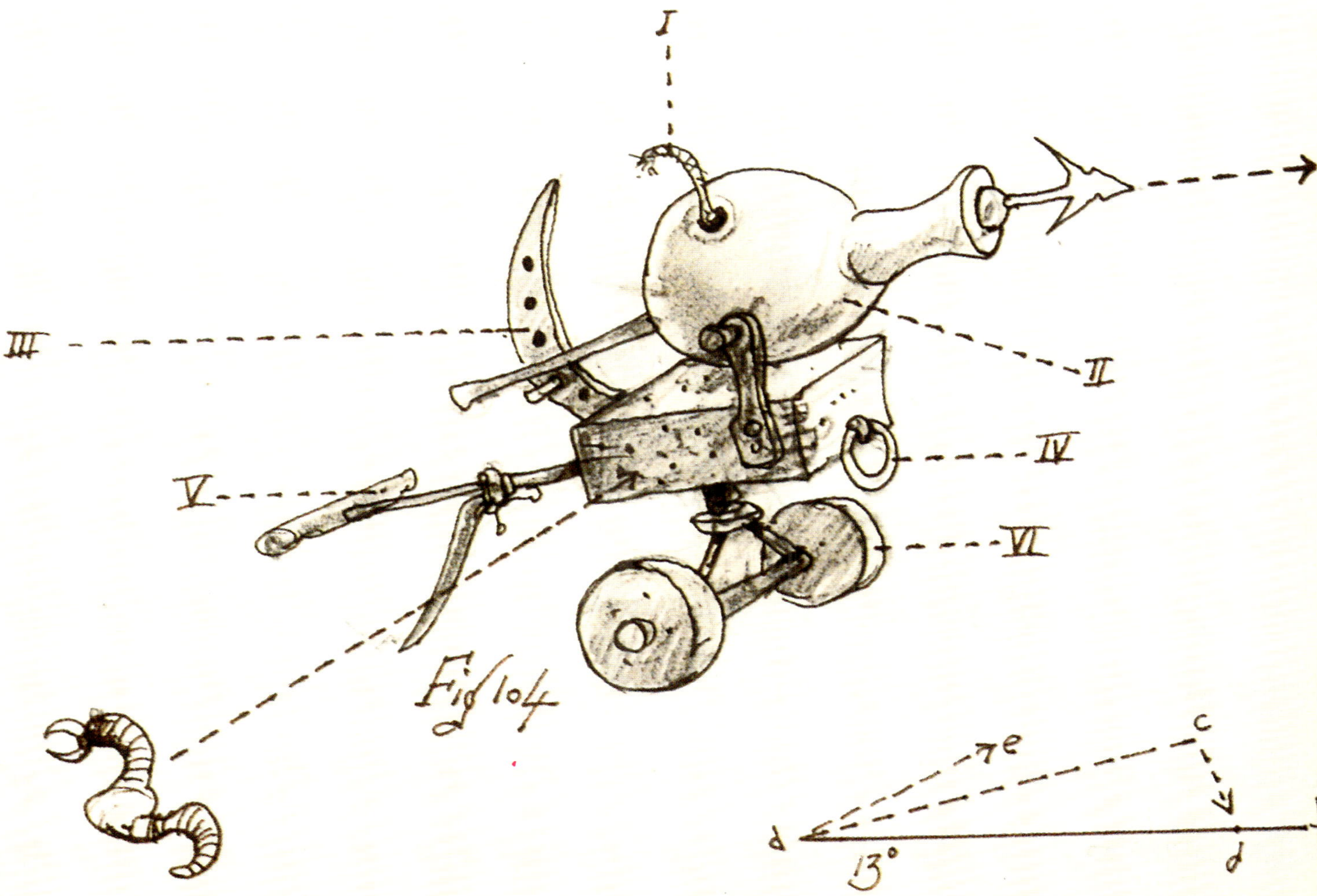
I
II
III
IV
V
VI
Fig 104
e
c
d
13°

Gröeg

Very little is known about this particular goblin. Some say it inhabits an imaginary world, where it wanders about confusing dreams and complicating people's glimpses of the Truth. Others believe that Gröeg is simply one of those mischievous little goblins that substitute margarine for the butter in the dish, or make you think you're about to drink a cup of tea when it's really coffee. Whatever its true nature, one can safely say that Gröeg lurks on the fringes of awareness and is always late for his lunch.

Gröeg is also credited with having had a part in the Great Collapse of Good Governance in the Labyrinth (see pages 18, 62, 64, and 66) although, once again, no one is quite sure which part.

GRÖEG

PLATE 35

Dogsthörpe

The great goblin detective, who solved so many baffling cases and tracked down so many do-gooders,* Dogsthörpe is also a byword in the Labyrinth for his total inability to hold a rational conversation with anybody. Even the most brilliant goblin conversationalists of his day have been unable to get anything out of him beyond the odd whine and the occasional bark.

Some believe that the part of the Dogsthörpe's brain that is capable of making rational conversation is missing. Others say that it's just because most of the brilliant conversationalists of the day are dead boring. To all this, however, his many fans and admirers have a simple reply: "Woof!"

**Do-gooders*: Being nice to somebody or doing someone a good turn is, of course, one of the most serious offences under the Prevention of Benevolence Act (1451), which was passed soon after the Great Collapse of Good Governance in the Labyrinth (see pages 18, 62, 64, 66, and 76).

Brêgg the Poet

Brêgg the poet is greatly admired and loved throughout the Labyrinth. Perhaps he is the single most admired and loved goblin there has ever been, and yet, oddly enough, he is also the most pitied, for he is haunted by a doppelgänger, or familiar, by the name of Fitch. This Fitch is, in itself, perfectly harmless, but it is also given to nibbling the hideously smelling Yeurrrrrrrch! root (fig. 5c). The odour that this vegetable gives off (particularly when nibbled in a special way) is so offensive that no goblin will go within three miles of it. (And one goblin mile is equal to fifty-nine of ours!) And so, since Fitch is never found not nibbling a Yeurrrrrrrch! root, poor Brêgg, though admired and loved, is forever shunned by all the other goblins of the Labyrinth.

Brêgg's most famous and least shunned* poem is the one addressed to the invisible egg of the Twark (see page 54).

* Even some of Brêgg's poems smell of the evil Yeurrrrrrrch! root.

"Ode to a Twark's Egg"

From the humble Twark you come, or do you?
O, Egg, I seem to see right through you!
You are like a Night-Troll's† visit.
That is so quiet, so brief, so is it?

Do you exist, O Twark's Egg, tell me?
If not, how is it I can smell thee?
Nay! I can taste thee from afar ... Hey!
Just whose corduroy trousers are they?‡

As you can see, goblin poetry is not all that good.

†For Night-Troll, see Septimüs, page 112.
‡Corduroy trousers—this is the smell of the Twark's egg (see page 54).

DO G STHÖRPE
BRÊGG
TÅTL ER
Fig. 5c

BØNÜS EVENTÜS
H
i
ii
iii
iv
d
KLÜN KIT
b
c

Bønüs Eventüs

Perhaps the least liked goblin in the whole Labyrinth is Bønüs Eventüs. The reason is that various bits of his body *talk* ... incessantly. His elbow (fig. i), for example, chatters on and on about the price of Kluttons' eggs (see fig. 129d and Klutton,* below) and how much cheaper they used to be when the Kluttons were allowed to sell them direct to the public ... *and* they tasted better, but that's because of the rubbish (see below) they feed the Kluttons on nowadays ... and so on and so on.... His fist (fig. ii) is a real pain in the neck (as it were), forever threatening other goblins with foreclosing on their mortgages, or telling everyone about what they had a bath in the night before, or threatening legal procedures if they put their hands to their heads in a certain way. His croutons† (fig. iii) sing operatic selections from all the worst goblin composers and screech abstracts from scientific journals in a language nobody understands, while his left foot (fig. iv) (as you'd expect) complains continually about being trodden on. The constant uproar that attends Bønüs Eventüs, wherever he goes, is deafening and exceedingly irritating, and it is not surprising that all goblins avoid him like the Plague.‡

**Klutton*: The unfortunate Klutton is probably the most unlucky bird in creation. It lays an egg three times as large as itself (see Bec and Cäül, page 50). This unbearably painful process is accompanied by such pathetic, heart-rending, and deafening squawks from the wretched creature that no goblin is prepared to live anywhere near a Klutton farm (except Bønüs Eventüs, see above). Even more unfortunate (if you happen to be a Klutton yourself) is the fact that in the natural state they lay their eggs four times a day! But there is worse to come. ... The eggs taste (faintly) of a goblin clothing material similar to worsted, which offers little gastronomic temptation to most goblins *but*—unfortunately for the Klutton—if the eggs are fried together in sufficient quantities (say four or five thousand at a time) and then sat on by any heavily rear-armoured goblin (such as Klünkit, on page 83), a minute quantity of hallucinogenic liquor is expressed. This liquor is esteemed so highly by goblins that they have developed intensive farming techniques for Kluttons. Klutton-farming has reached the point now where the poor Kluttons are induced to lay thirty or forty eggs a day! Farm Kluttons become prematurely old and lose their feathers and *joie de vivre* within moments of birth.

In happier times, Kluttons were friendly, helpful, hardworking little birds. They managed their own affairs, kept their accounts in order, took their eggs to market themselves (no inconsiderable feat, considering the size of the eggs) and sold them direct to the public. Some goblins believe that the degradation of the Klutton, in pursuit of the hallucinogenic liquor from its egg, was directly responsible for the Great Collapse of Good Governance in the Labyrinth (see pages 18, 62, 64, 66, 76, and 78). There have even been movements for reform, such as: the Society for the Prevention of Cruelty to Kluttons, the Society for the Reduction of Klutton Despair, the Royal Society for the Cheering-up of Distressed Kluttons, Ban the Klutton Farm Yesterday Action Group, and so on. Unfortunately for the Kluttons, the miserable bird eats rubbish, and no goblin government has been prepared to eradicate the wretched Klutton Farms, for fear of ending up with a refuse crisis. As I say, the Klutton must be the most unfortunate bird in creation.

†*Croutons*: These form a portion of the goblin anatomy which has no counterpart in human anatomy. It is perhaps most like the human tonsil, but not very.

‡The Plague that hit the Labyrinth shortly after the Great Collapse of Good Governance was a strange one. It was a Plague of Laughter, Cackles, and Acute Sniggering. It affected some 90 percent of the goblin population, but was, fortunately, only fatal in odd cases—such as for goblins who had a Chuckle Allergy or those who kept kipper-filleting equipment in their noses .

PLATE 36

Klünkit

Klünkit is one of the rear-armoured goblins mentioned in the previous entry (see page 82). Of course, like all rear-armoured goblins, Klünkit goes into battle backwards and is always more dangerous in retreat than attack. His inside leg measurement is unknown and—more to the point—irrelevant.

Låmpsöniüs

Låmpsöniüs is, along with the Cändlewic (page 34) and Agmǿür (page 103), one of the Keepers of the Goblin Hoard. Day and night they stand on guard ... day in ... day out ... never sleeping ... never eating ... never taking holidays ... never taking weekend breaks to get away from it all. ... How do they keep at it? Nobody knows. What do they live on? We can only guess. How do they remain so ever vigilant? No one can even start to begin to conceive. But perhaps the biggest riddle of them all is the one that will never be answered: What is the Goblin Hoard a hoard of? Not even *they* have the faintest idea.

LÅMPS ÖNIÜS

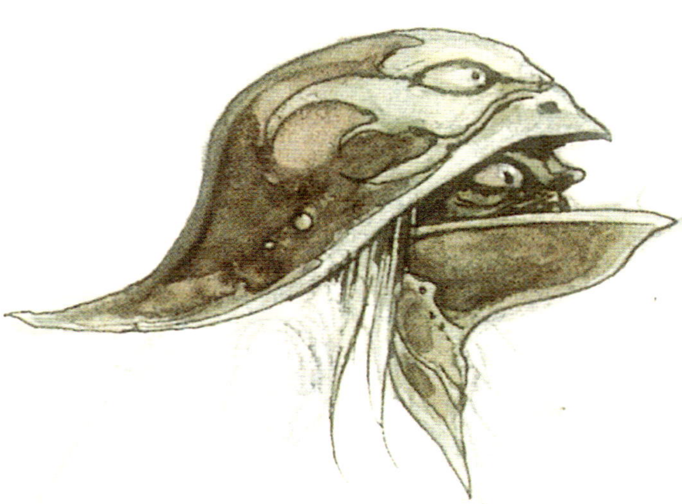

Feedle

Feedle is one of the many Bandit Goblins who inhabit the High Hills beyond the Labyrinth. Given to raping and plundering though he is, Feedle is remarkable amongst such goblins for his unconventional attitude to what he steals. Although a ruthless and vicious killer, Feedle always returns stolen goods. Not only does he return them, but he has them burnished-up good as new (see Gürdy, page 66) and writes a little note on them to the owner (even if he has murdered the owner in cold blood) wishing him good luck in future years and happiness in his fine possessions. He usually includes a little rhyme, such as:

Thank you for your crock of gold,
I hope you haven't caught a cold
Nor got too testy with your robber,
His name was Feedle that did you clobber.

Fig. II

For eating, Feedle usually dons a mask through which he sucks raw vegetables.

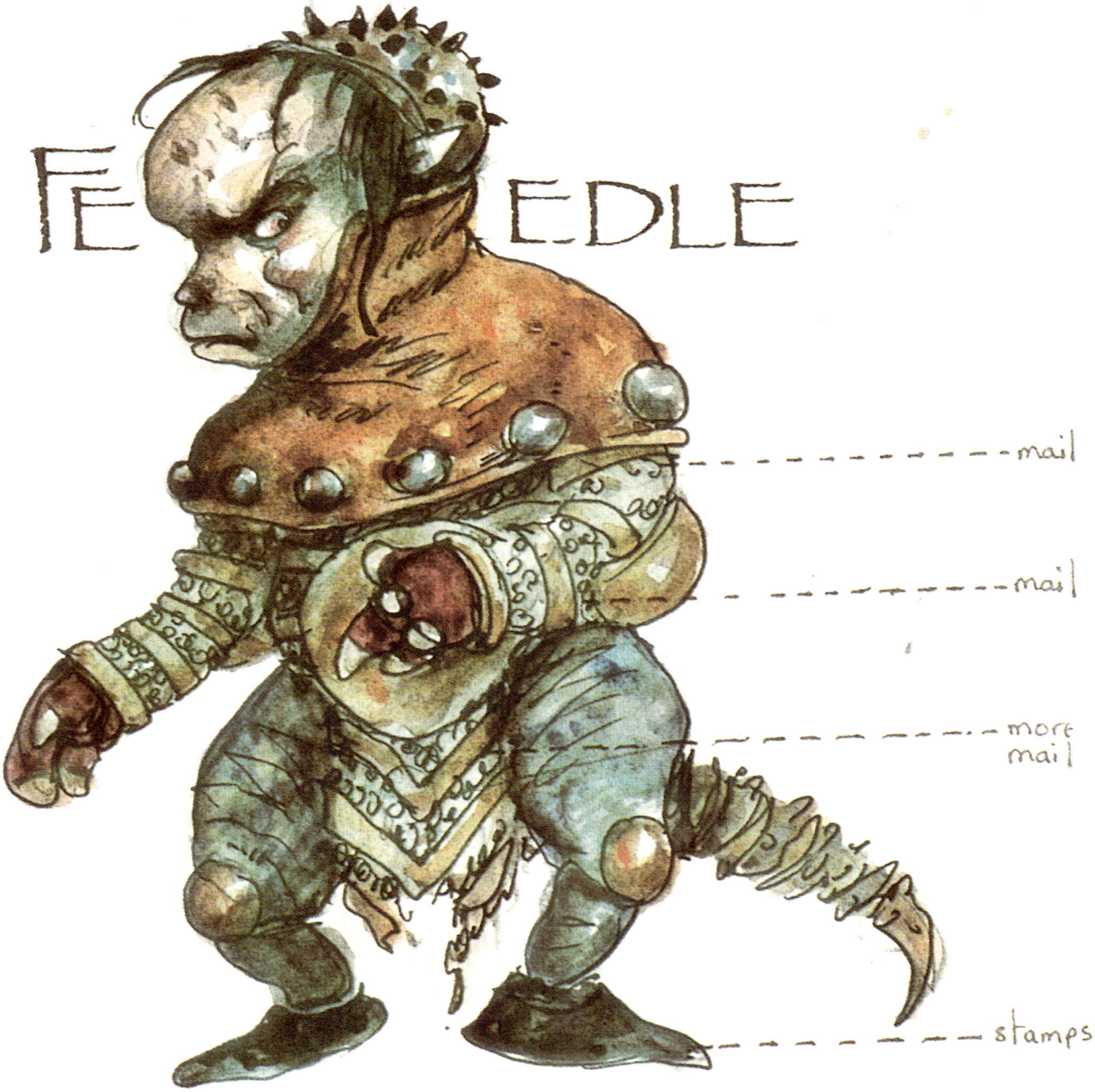
FE EDLE
mail
mail
more mail
stamps

Fig II

Weech

Weech—the Great Cook—is renowned not so much for the delicacy of her cooking as for the *quantity* of it! Weech has cooked single-handed for entire armies (often on opposing sides) ever since the Dawn of Goblinkind in the Labyrinth. Her method is simple and her cuisine is down-to-earth : Something Brown in a Brown Gravy is one of her staples. Occasionally she has cooked more elaborate dishes such as Something Brown in a Brown Gravy with Some Other Blackish-Brown Bits Scraped Off the Side. Once or twice she has experimented with the *nouvelle cuisine* style of cooking, such as when she prepared a dish beautifully arranged on the plate and called it Something Brown Without Even Any Brown Gravy. This last was not popular amongst goblins. In fact, goblins in general prefer her feast-day blow-outs such as Two Brown Things in a Brown Gravy with Another Brown Thing on Top—Twice.

Although capable of cooking for entire armies single-handed, Weech is normally helped by her assistant, Stench (see below).

Stench

The Great Cook's Assistant

There are very few parts of Stench's body that do not drip, dribble, ooze, run, leak, trickle, seep, or weep some sort of waste matter, pus, or suppuration. Weech, the Great Cook, however, swears that he is essential to all her culinary endeavours. And many goblins say that it is true that on the few days when Stench, the Great Cook's Assistant, has been laid low by running sores and boils, the food has certainly tasted different.

According to Weech, she likes to use Stench as an assistant because he always puts his whole heart into the cooking (fig. 10). Fortunately, he always takes it out again, but, she says, it does add that *je ne sais quoi*.

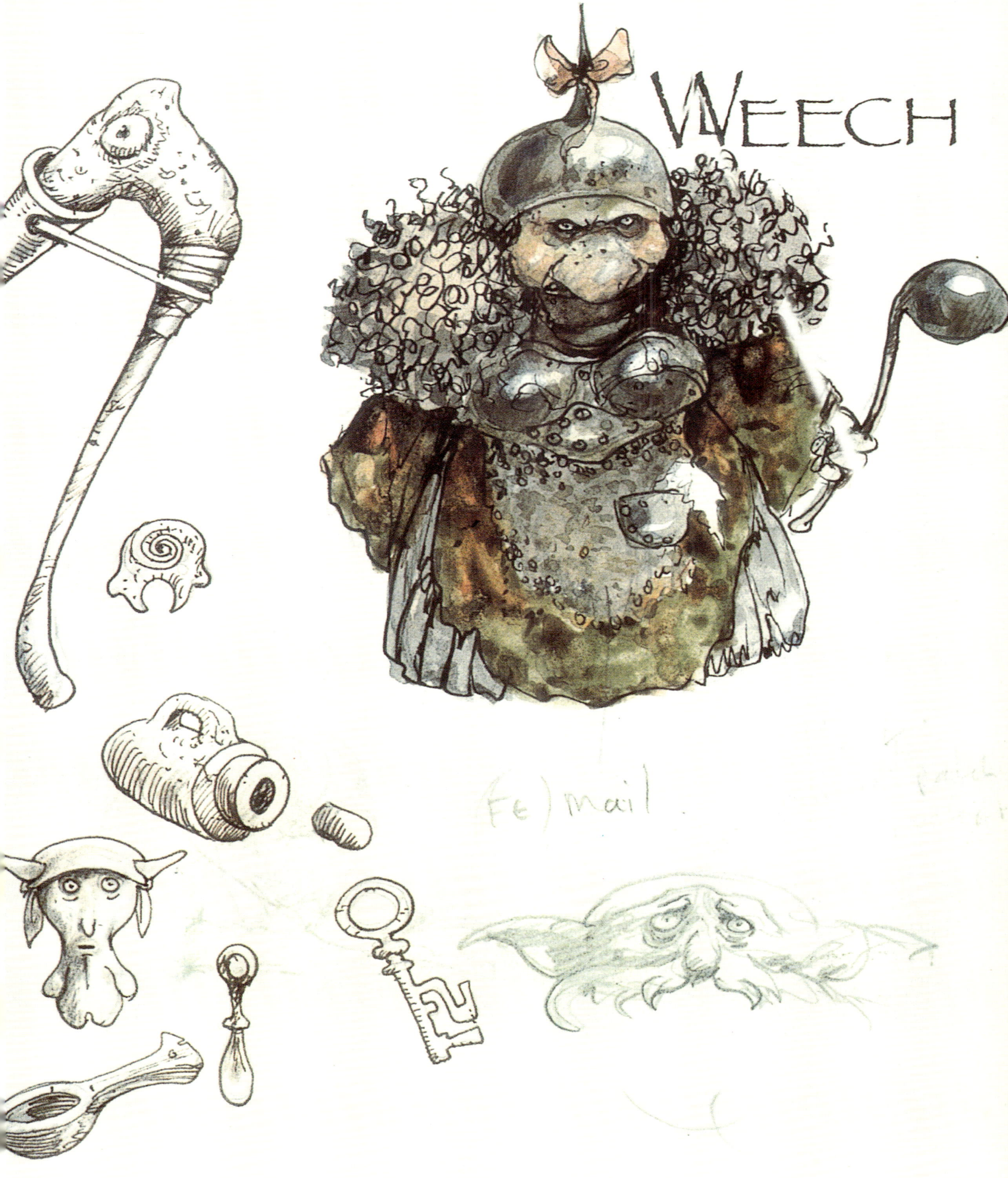
WEECH
Fe) mail

Smoakes
.76
53
STE
NCH
pöng!
drip
Chain mail
boils
Back flap
tarnish
dribbles
drips
Toes turn in
Fig 10.

Løch

Løch is a venerable old goblin with a reputation for wisdom and sound judgement. How he acquired this reputation is anyone's guess, yet he proceeds through the Labyrinth with his usher, Ness, holding court and pronouncing judgement on his fellow goblins.

Many of Løch's judgements have become proverbial. On one occasion, for example, he was asked to mediate between Tr̂ysöp (see page 40) and Frölöw (see page 42) as to whether or not Frölöw had just eaten Tr̂ysöp's heart. The Old Judge Løch sat in silence for a long time—some say it was seventy days and seventy nights—and when he finally opened his eyes, he found that everyone had gone home. So he and Ness continued on their way and never heard from either Tr̂ysöp or Frölöw again. This is typical of the sort of pointless stories that goblins love to tell each other.

Ness

Usher to the Old Judge Løch (for which, see above).

Ness
Løch

B-713K

Gentle and home-loving creatures, the B-713Ks are tamed by goblins. They sing charmingly and can be taught to talk.

There is one snag, however.... The B-713Ks have absolutely no sense of humour, and a casual greeting such as "Hi, Beaky!" or a friendly comment on how much their birdseed costs is liable to be misconstrued, and many an unfortunate goblin owner has had his head snipped off with one clean snap of those razor sharp claws. Not a pet for the faint-hearted or those with squeamish mothers.

B-713K

Nìve

FØRWKE

Nive

Nive and his partner, Førwke, have, of course, long been in the avant-garde of goblin fashion design. Their brilliant spring collections draw admiring crowds from the length and breadth of the Labyrinth. Sometimes shocking, sometimes outrageous, often breathtakingly original but more often delightful redefinitions of traditional designs, their creations always have one thing in common—nobody ever wears them. ... Perhaps they are too expensive (the price tags are not only enormous but unremovable) ... perhaps no one is bold enough to be seen in public wearing such designs (well, you try wandering around town with an eight-foot price tag sticking out of your collar) ... or perhaps the clothes are simply too heavy (polished granite embroidered with lead piping is one of their favourite materials) ... but whatever the reason, the simple fact is that the fabulous and famous Nive and Førwke have never sold a single suit of clothes and are desperately hard up. If you can't send gold just send food, as they are constantly on the edge of starvation. They repeatedly refuse to design clothes for goblins fatter than themselves. Note the line and flair of these particular creations (c, d, b).

Førwke

See Nive above. Note points IV, II, I, and III, but not in that order.

Börgis Khån

Long ago, from across the Terrible Howling Gulf came Börgis Khån the Conqueror, the Leader of the Goblin Multitudes, the Cruel Avenger of Fate. He and his hordes swept down across the Plain of Plenty and through the Labyrinth deep into the heart of Goblin City, wreaking havoc and destruction wherever they went. It was then, however, that Börgis Khån met his match, Gibbergeist, the tragedian and tripe-bugler (see page 36).

Gibbergeist was in the full throes of one of his famous extended death sequences and was not going to be upstaged by any Cruel Avenger of Fate or any Marauding Horde. He therefore continued acting out his agonizing and protracted death for the benefit of his now genuinely terrified audience. Börgis Khån had never seen a theatrical performance before (coming from the other side of the terrible Howling Gulf) and was totally taken in by the horrendous (and lengthy) spectacle of the great tragedian dying. When Gibbergeist finally appeared to give up the ghost, Börgis Khån ventured forwards to touch the gown of one who had died in such agony. Whereupon Gibbergeist the tragedian leapt up into the air and performed an encore as his own ghost. The unsuspecting Börgis Khån was so terrified out of his wits that he raced back across the Plain of Plenty, over the Terrible Howling Gulf, and was never seen again.

BÖRGIS
KHÅN

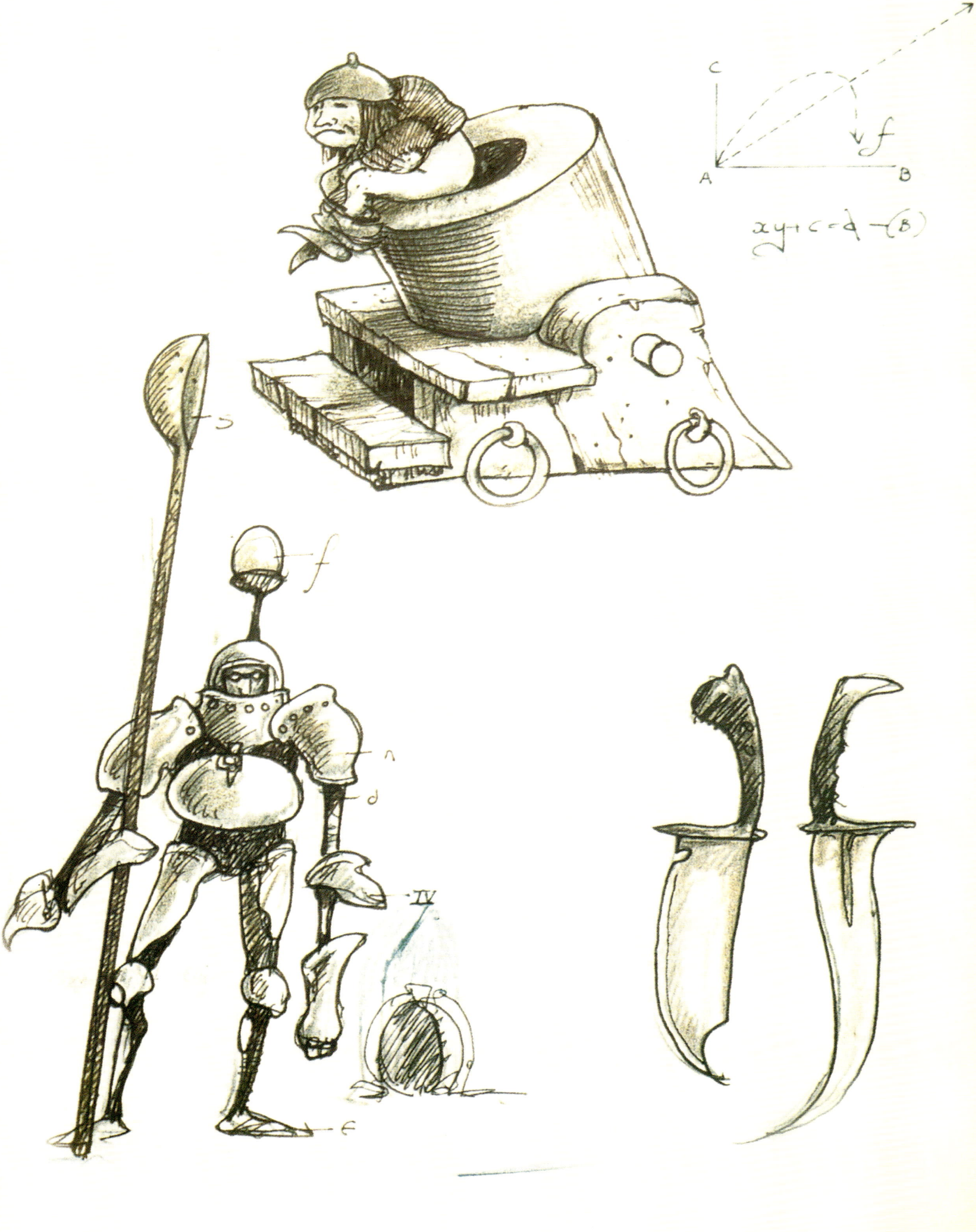
C
f
A
B
IV

Loading the Big Bertha

This is a goblin tradition on the eve of battle. It is written down in *The Book of Time** that the first shot of battle shall always be non-fatal ... but unpleasant.

**The Book of Time*: In this book are enshrined many of the Goblin Laws that were observed prior to the Great Collapse of Good Governance in the Labyrinth (see pages 18, 62, 64, 66, 76, and 78).

Goblin Tournaments

These usually take place on Feast and Fight Days, such as the Day of Beyond Reckoning or the Day of Alger Öt (see page 118), as well, of course, as the Night of Ten Thousand Joys and Toe-Feast Night (for which, see above, somewhere or other). The object of the jousting is to dislodge the opponent's egg (fig. f), scrape it off the ground, scramble it, and make it into an omelette sandwich. Goblins who have recently pointed at the Blessed "I" on the holy relic in the Silent Sepulchre are, of course, automatically disqualified (see fig. VII, page 49).

Agmøür

One of the Keepers of the Goblin Hoard along with Cändlewic (page 34) and Låmpsöniüs (page 84).

Aêlst

One of the great goblin *skalds* or Tale-Tellers, Aêlst is much sought after to entertain at feasts and banquets. His store of ballads, yarns, anecdotes, chronicles, fables, epics, quips, sagas, histories, elegies, satires, legends, romances, adventures, sketches, and tales of battle is seemingly interminable—as indeed are the stories themselves. Another thing that distinguishes the compositions of Aêlst from those of almost any other *skald* or Tale-Teller is the fact that he *never* uses more than a dozen different words. To some extent this economical use of language explains the impression of interminableness induced by his recitations. The twelve words he uses are: *lump*, *sparrow*, *like*, *the*, *was*, *roaring*, *gusset*, *scuff*, *limp*, *testy*, *bitten-off*, and *rubbish*.

Grüempy

Grüempy is one of the Snatter Goblins that live deep in the crevices of the Labyrinth's brickwork. He and his cousins and brothers and sisters scamper out to snatter* when the moon shines. Although snattering was officially banned at the 1000th All-Goblin Certitude Convention, the practice still persists wherever there is brickwork in the Labyrinth.

**To snatter*: This is a favourite goblin activity. It involves scampering out of the Labyrinth's brickwork when the moon shines and then scampering back in again with a cry of "Snatterers of the World! Voice your doubts!"

AGMØÜR

Aêlst

Grüempy

Müskül

Müskül is an Edible Goblin of the genus *Goblinus goblinis edibilis.* The edibility of goblins is a vexed question. Some authorities hold that all goblins are poisonous, but there are families where generation upon generation have eaten goblin and apparently thrived on it. I myself know of one such family. The trick is first of all to recognize the edible variety, which is distinguishable by its tusk, its helmet, and its bad breath. Not *all* parts of the Edible Goblin, however, are safe to eat, and it is essential that the cook knows which parts are and which parts aren't. The body and limbs are, of course, deadly poisonous, but certain parts of the head are delicious when marinated in a little mulberry wine and turpentine. (It's a pity that the turpentine is also poisonous.) However, for those who wish to try this delicacy, here is the key to the Edible Goblin Chart on plate 50, fig. 3.

b: Edible but not very nice.
f: Inedible and not very nice.
36: Edible provided you like being sick.
9: Edible but not very nice.
10: Inedible.
4: Deadly poisonous. If taken accidentally, phone the ambulance *and* the mortuary. The person who ate it will need the latter, and everyone who touches the corpse will need the former!
2: Deadly poisonous. If eaten it attacks the digestive juices, liver, and kidneys and finally produces distressing and fatal wind which will render a square mile around its victim uninhabitable for several hundred years.
3: Edible but not very nice.
64: Delicious! Perhaps one of the most tantalizing and delicate flavours that will ever touch your palate. Unfortunately it will also be the last since it, too, is deadly poisonous.
11: Edible but a bit like chewing one of the exhibits at Madame Tussaud's. (I'm not allowed to say which one...)
19: Edible but leads to discoloration of the skin—tending to make most people bright purple.
?: Edibility unknown.
104: Edible—especially good for those who like to see their food three or four times.
13: Edible but scarcely worth the effort.
11: Deadly poisonous unless your name is Valerie.
27: Edible, schmedible.
94: Edible, but should only be consumed when there's nothing else on offer.

TUSK (for identification purposes only)
a: a soft brown colour, shiny and vile smelling.
b: bifurcated root, pale pinkish-grey and vile smelling.

Müs
KÜL
Fig 3
b
36
2
9
11
19
4
64
3
104
?
13
94
27
11
10
f
a
b

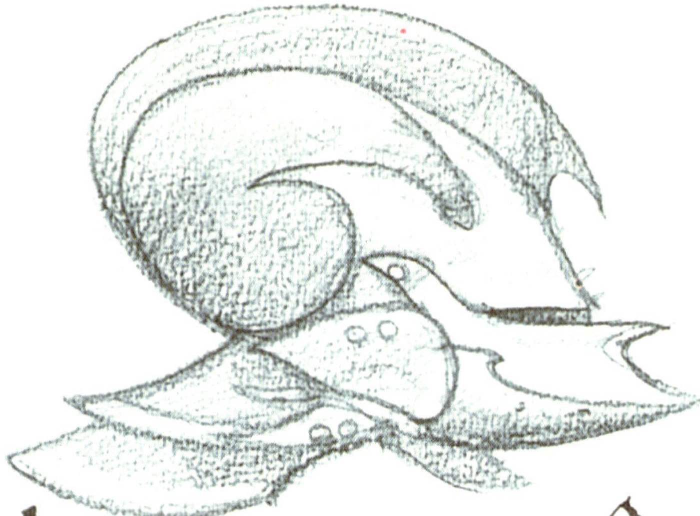

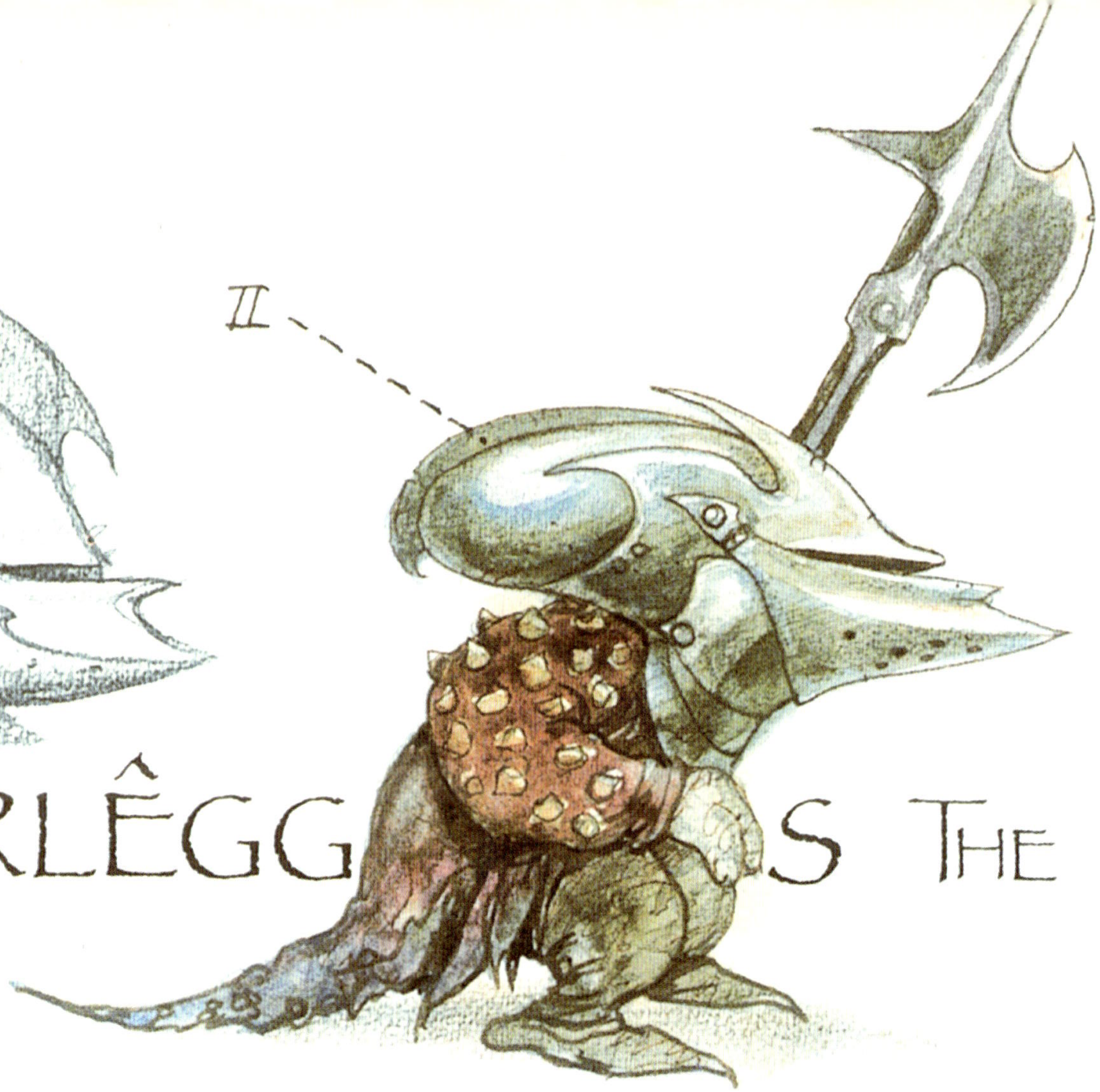

Lætherlêggs the Löw

Lætherlêggs the Löw

The Tale of Lætherlêggs

Once upon a time, there was a tall, handsome goblin by the name of Lætherlêggs the Lofty. He was proud and carried his helmet on his arm so that all the goblin maidens could see his face and swoon over him, which they always did. He would strut about on the ramparts of the goblin castles and show off his legs and tail, and all the other goblins hated him.

Then one day an insignificant goblin by the name of Alger Öt decided to teach Lætherlêggs the Lofty a lesson.

Alger Öt crept into the castle where Lætherlêggs the Lofty was preening himself on the ramparts before a group of admirers. Alger Öt climbed to the top of the North East Tower and stuck his head over the side and called:

"My word! Lætherlêggs you do look small from up here!"

"Come down at once!" cried out Lætherlêggs the Lofty. "You know I can't bear anyone being higher than me!"

"You look no taller than the lowest measure on Hörtenz's dipstick!"* shouted Alger Öt.

"Don't say things like that!" cried out Lætherlêggs.

"Go away!" shouted his admirers. "You'll make him cry!"

"You look even smaller than a Twark's egg!"† called out Alger Öt, who was beginning to enjoy himself for the very first time in his life.

"Oh! Shut up!" said several more of Lætherlêggs' admirers, who had run up the stairs of the Tower and now suddenly appeared behind Alger Öt, seized him by his scruffy neck, and threw him over the parapet.

*See Hörtenz, page 52.

†See Twark, page 54.

Alger Öt gave the most awful scream, but Lætherlêggs the Lofty had his face buried in his hanky, crying his eyes out, and he didn't look up once ... and this was his undoing. For Alger Öt came hurtling down so fast that he would certainly have laid Lætherlêggs low had he struck him. But he didn't.... He just missed hitting Lætherlêggs on the crown of his helmet (fig. II) and landed instead in the moat. Alger Öt's scream, however, surprised an Amâm Pherrüginüs that happened to be flying overhead.‡ It was put off its stroke for a moment, then totally forgot all its flying technique and plummeted out of the sky. To the horror of the assembled admirers the Amâm landed fair and square on the crown of Lætherlêggs the Lofty's head (fig. II) and compacted him into a ridiculously short and stumpy figure. And from that day to this he has been called Lætherlêggs the Löw. As for Alger Öt, he was none the worse for his ducking, and all the other goblins (apart from Lætherlêggs's admirers) were so pleased with what he'd done they held a feast to celebrate, and they still do every year on the Day of Alger Öt (see Goblin Tournaments, page 102).

‡For the Amâm Pherrüginüs, see page 38.

Septimüs

Septimüs is a typical Night-Troll. He steals silently and stealthily around people's gardens and under bridges when the stars and moon are hidden by clouds and night is thickest. He is a terrifying and unnerving sight, or rather he would be if you ever saw him, but he is so silent and so stealthy and his visits so brief that nobody ever knows he's there or even not there (see Brêgg the Poet's "Ode to a Twark's Egg," page 79) ... and *that's* the worrying part.

Septì müs

Böegiböe

The Tale of Böegiböe

Böegiböe travelled over the High Hills. He carried his staff in one hand and in the other he carried nothing.

"Where are you going so wild and free, Böegiböe?" asked Aksark the Gypsy.

"I am going to fill my other hand," replied Böegiböe.

"I can tell you where you can find fennel flowers and willow herbs, forget-me-do's and baby's beard, plants to make you well, plants to make you sleep, plants to heal the wounds of your mind. Those will fill your other hand."

"No," said Böegiböe. "That's not good enough for me." And he went on his way.

Some time later he came to the Great Howling Gulf, and beside the Great Howling Gulf he came across Lod the Conjurer.

"Böegiböe!" cried Lod the Conjurer. "Where are you going so free and fast?"

"I am going to fill my other hand," replied Böegiböe.

"Stay here with me," said Lod the Conjurer, "and I will give you dice and cards, disappearing rabbits and magic snakes, multiplying handkerchieves and clever hoops—*they'll* fill your other hand."

"No," said Böegiböe. "That's not good enough for me." And he went on his way.

Some time later he came to the goblin castle that stands by the rich red lake. And there he met Haza, the fat maid, who is forever carried about by her servant.

"Böegiböe!" cried Haza. "Where are you going so free and furious?"

"I am going to fill my other hand," replied Böegiböe.

"Stay here with me," replied Haza, "and I will give you rubies and riches, gold and silver, pearls and amethysts, pleasures and purchases.... *They'll* fill your other hand for you."

"No," said Böegiböe. "That's not good enough for me." And he turned to go, but as he did so, he heard a splash followed by a crash, and there was Alger Öt struggling in the castle moat.

"Help!" cried Alger Öt. "I can't swim!"

Böegiböe rushed down to the moatside and stretched out his hand. Alger Öt grabbed it just as he was about to sink for the third time, and Böegiböe pulled him to safety. Then a crowd gathered around them and told Alger Öt that Lætherlêggs the Lofty had been hit by an Amåm Pherrüginüs and was now Lætherlêggs the Löw. Then they all cheered and Alger Öt shook Böegiböe by the hand, and as he did so, Böegiböe looked down at his hand and said: "That's good enough for me," and Böegiböe and Alger Öt became friends for the rest of their lives. As I say, goblins like pointless stories.

Böe Gìböe

ALGERÖT

Alger Öt

For Alger Öt, see the *Tale of Lætherlêggs*, page 110, and the *Tale of Böegiböe*, page 114.

Fowler

Trusted by no one, shunned by everyone, feared and despised in equal proportions, Fowler sneaks his way through the Labyrinth with his nets and snares. Each little bird or small goblin that he traps he sticks in his bag and takes ... no one knows where. Nobody knows where or when he will strike next ... but strike he will and he will ensnare us all in time.

FOWLER

Dåshe

It is thanks to the quick pencil of Dåshe that we have any portraits at all of any of the goblins. It was the discovery of Dåshe's notebooks (forty-three in all) containing lightning portraits of his friends and contemporaries that enabled Brian Froud, the human artist (see page 121), to render the representations of the goblins that you see in this volume.

Phester

A very unpleasant goblin. Being very small, he is capable of climbing into an adult animal's open sore, entering the bloodstream, going once around the system and out again, leaving a small trace in the heart that creates the impression of being in love—but with no particular object for your affection. Most unsettling.

Brian Froud

The Human Artist

Little did Brian Froud think, when he undertook this work, that he would encounter so much opposition from the goblins themselves. Suffice it to say that he found it necessary to don armour. But even then he found himself unable to deal with the concerted attempts of goblins to wreck his work by forcing him to drink more and more really good wine, and then, while he was otherwise occupied, crawling across his pages with inky feet.

Prematurely aged, the artist finally gave up in despair and abandoned his work to the goblins themselves ... and to the Pouilly Fuissé....

Spürgüs

The Happiest Goblin. The Skating Goblin. A Goblin with No Problems. A Goblin of Hope. Spürgüs is always the last goblin in any roll call of goblin names, for the simple reason that he doesn't give a hoot!

DÅSHE

PHESTER

F
H
A
D
B
P
iv
j
L
N
h

SPÜRG
ÜS

Bec & Cåwl

Cousins of Bec and Cäül (see page 50). They are a miserable pair whose only mission in life is to stop Spürgüs the Skating Goblin from being the last name in this book. But they can't succeed, because the last name is *always* that of Spürgüs.

Bec
&
Cåwl

white
blue
brown